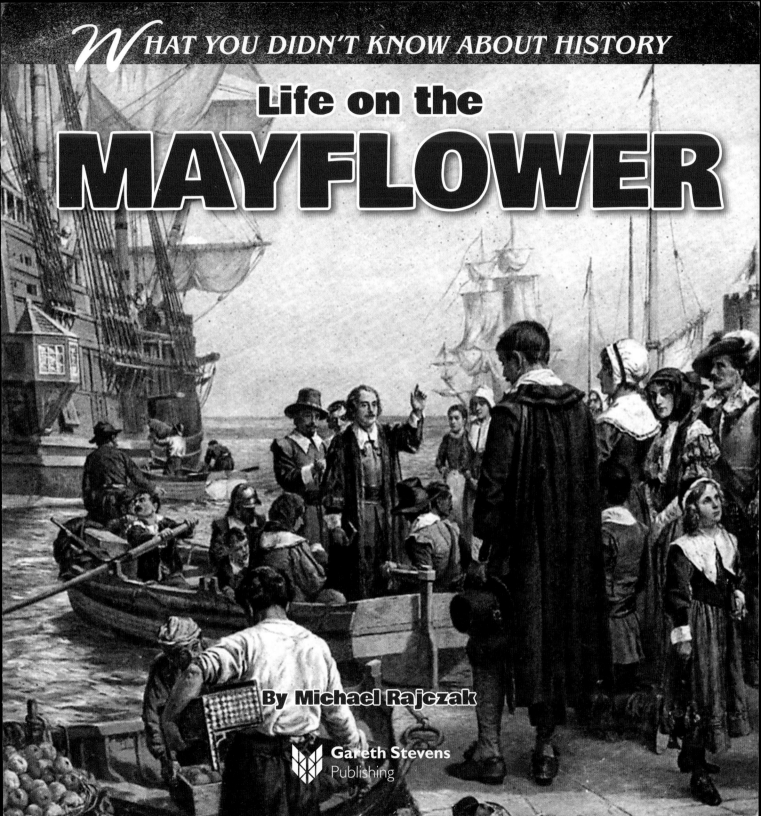

Life on the
MAYFLOWER

By Michael Rajczak

Gareth Stevens
Publishing

Please visit our website, www.garethstevens.com. For a free color catalog of all our high-quality books, call toll free 1-800-542-2595 or fax 1-877-542-2596.

Library of Congress Cataloging-in-Publication Data

Rajczak, Michael.
Life on the Mayflower / by Michael Rajczak.
  p. cm. — (What you didn't know about history)
Includes index.
ISBN 978-1-4824-0592-7 (pbk.)
ISBN 978-1-4824-0594-1 (6-pack)
ISBN 978-1-4824-0591-0 (library binding)
1. Pilgrims (New Plymouth Colony) — Juvenile literature. 2. Mayflower (Ship) — Juvenile literature. 3. Massachusetts — History — New Plymouth, 1620-1691 — Juvenile literature. I. Rajczak, Michael. II. Title.
F68.R35 2014
974.402—dc23

First Edition

Published in 2014 by
Gareth Stevens Publishing
111 East 14th Street, Suite 349
New York, NY 10003

Designer: Andrea Davison-Bartolotta
Editor: Kristen Rajczak

Photo credits: Cover, p. 1 Universal History Archive/Getty Images; p. 9 MPI/Getty Images; p. 5 American School/The Bridgeman Art Library/Getty Images; p. 7 Ron Embleton/The Bridgeman Art Library/Getty Images; p. 8 Three Lions/Getty Images; p. 10 VisitBritain/ Britain on View/Getty Images; p. 11 (inset) DEA Picture Library/De Agostini Picture Library/ Getty Images; p. 11 (background) iStockphoto/Thinkstock; p. 13 Peter Ptschelinzew/Lonely Planet Images/Getty Images; p. 15 (main) Richard Nowitz/National Geographic/Getty Images; p. 15 (inset) Dorling Kindersley RF/Thinkstock; p. 16 Hemera/Thinkstock; p. 17 John Nordell/The Christian Science Monitor via Getty Images; p. 19 (inset) © iStockphoto.com/Berryspun; p. 19 (main) Spirit of America/Shutterstock.com.

Printed in the United States of America

CPSIA compliance information: Batch #CW14GS: For further information contact Gareth Stevens, New York, New York at 1-800-542-2595.

CONTENTS

Words in the glossary appear in **bold** type the first time they are used in the text.

WHAT IS A PILGRIM?

A pilgrim is someone who goes on a journey, often for **religious** reasons. We call the group of people who settled Plymouth Colony in 1620 Pilgrims, and religion was one of the reasons they traveled on the *Mayflower* to the **New World**.

Some of the Pilgrims were Separatists, a religious group that wanted to separate from the official Church of England. But following other faiths was illegal in England! Some Separatists were thrown into crowded jails. Others escaped to the Netherlands in the early 1600s.

Did You Know?

Other Separatist groups included some Baptists and Quakers. The Quakers and their leader William Penn founded the colony of Pennsylvania.

Separatist groups left for the Netherlands because that country allowed people to practice whatever religion they wanted.

WHY START A NEW LIFE?

The Separatists lived in the Netherlands for about 11 years, but they didn't find happiness. Most worked hard jobs for little pay. They were troubled that their children were learning Dutch **customs** and slowly losing their English way of life.

The Separatists made a deal with the Virginia Company to settle in the Hudson River valley. There they hoped to have religious freedom while keeping their English background and language. King James I allowed it—he was just happy to be rid of the troublemakers!

Did You Know?

When it came time to chart the *Mayflower*'s course, a northern route was chosen. This was because pirates were more active in the warmer waters toward the south.

The Pilgrims didn't want to join those already settled at Jamestown Colony. They worried the colonists there would have a problem with their religion, just like people in England did.

7

THE PASSENGERS

Though the Separatists are the most well known of the Pilgrims, other passengers also traveled on the *Mayflower*. Some wanted to start businesses, such as fishing. Others were hired laborers or household servants. The Separatists called these other passengers "strangers."

Illness and rough seas didn't help the groups befriend each other. There were disagreements throughout the journey. When the *Mayflower*'s main mast was smashed in a storm, the passengers and crew argued about whether the *Mayflower* was safe to sail.

Did You Know?
The Separatists called themselves "saints."

Only 37 of the 102 Pilgrims on the Mayflower were Separatists. Rats, cockroaches, and disgusting flies shared the journey, too.

THE MAYFLOWER

The *Mayflower* was a **merchant** ship used to haul goods such as furs, iron, and wine. The Pilgrims' **voyage** would be the first and only passenger trip for the *Mayflower*.

Not much is known about what the *Mayflower* looked like. It was probably about 100 feet (30 m) long and 24 feet (7 m) wide, with six main sails and three masts. However, it's known that *Mayflower* was a common name for English ships, so the Pilgrims' *Mayflower* wasn't the only one!

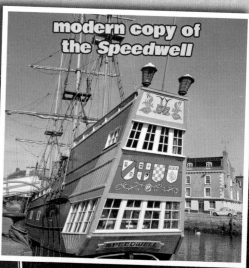

modern copy of the *Speedwell*

Did You Know?

The Pilgrims planned on traveling in two ships, the *Mayflower* and the *Speedwell*. The *Speedwell* sprang leaks early in the voyage, so the Pilgrims had to leave it behind, along with some of the passengers.

QUARTERS FOR PASSENGERS

The 102 passengers aboard the *Mayflower* had to live crowded between the main decks in an area usually full of **cargo**! Using blankets and what clothing they had, the Pilgrims made up beds on the hard deck floor. They were unprepared for such a rough trip.

When the waves tossed the *Mayflower* about, passengers suffered injuries from being thrown against the ship walls! Many people were often seasick. Even worse, there was no **privacy** and only a few **chamber pots** for everyone to share.

Did You Know?

Some of the passengers stayed in the ship's hold, the main storage place for supplies such as food, water, and baggage. It was only about 5 feet (1.5 m) high and smelled strongly of old wine from previous voyages.

A crossing of the Atlantic Ocean was considered a very dangerous journey in 1620. It was made even more unpleasant by rain and waves streaming into the areas where Pilgrims slept.

13

The *Mayflower* had a crew of about 30. The ship's master (captain) and owner was 50-year-old Christopher Jones. He died 2 years later, probably because of health problems that began on the voyage.

The rest of the crew included a cook, a doctor, and **pilot** John Clarke, who also piloted a ship bound for Jamestown in 1611! A carpenter handled repairs, and four men called quartermasters were in charge of the cargo and fishing gear. The boatswain took care of the sails and rigging, or ropes.

Did You Know?

Because they often threw up all over themselves, the sailors called the passengers "puke stockings." Freshwater was too **valuable** on board a ship to use for washing clothing.

**lookouts aboard
the *Mayflower***

15

Imagine being tossed and thrown about by waves and the motion of a moving ship all night. It doesn't sound very restful! There was little fresh air in the cargo holds, too. So, when seas were calm, some passengers would head to the top deck. But they only saw water as far as the eye could see.

Calm seas also meant a hot meal, commonly stew or peas porridge. However, most meals were served cold. The Pilgrims most often ate cheese, dried and salted meat, and biscuits.

Did You Know?

The water brought aboard the *Mayflower* became spoiled and was too sickening to drink. Everyone then had to drink beer.

beer barrel

A good day meant a meal of oatmeal or fish, but a bad day meant a stormy sea—and not much of an appetite.

17

CHILDREN ON BOARD

Life wasn't easy for children on the *Mayflower*. They only had a little space on the floor to sleep, eat, and play. When they could, it's likely the children played games such as tic-tac-toe, checkers, and marbles. When there was enough light for reading, children would read the Bible.

But the close quarters meant children got into trouble easily, usually because of being too loud or too active. Once, two brothers were playing with fire next to barrels filled with gunpowder!

Did You Know?

Elizabeth Hopkins was one of three pregnant women aboard the *Mayflower*. During the voyage, she gave birth to a son she named Oceanus.

Life aboard the Mayflower was often boring—and stinky—for children.

GUN POWDER XXX

19

ARE WE THERE YET?

After about 2,750 miles (4,425 km) and 66 days, Cape Cod in present-day Massachusetts was sighted at sunrise. The *Mayflower* was too far north, though! The Pilgrims had been hoping to settle at the mouth of the Hudson River where New York City is today.

As the Pilgrims tried to sail south, stormy ocean currents nearly overturned the ship! They decided it would be safer to stay around Cape Cod. They chose an old Native American settlement and named it Plymouth.

Did You Know?

The Pilgrims signed the Mayflower Compact aboard the ship before they settled the colony. It was a short agreement between all those on the ship to stick together—even though they didn't land where they were planning!

More Facts You Didn't Know About the *Mayflower!*

- Plymouth Colony was named after Plymouth, England, the place where the *Mayflower* began its voyage.

- The Pilgrims wore the same clothing for the whole trip—yuck!

- The *Mayflower* was armed! A gunner was in charge of the guns, cannon, and gunpowder.

- The final place chosen for settlement wasn't the only location the Pilgrims looked at. In fact, they sailed around the area of Cape Cod for weeks before choosing their spot.

- The Pilgrims weren't legally allowed to live at Plymouth until a few years after they'd landed. Their **charter** was for the land around the Hudson River—and that's it.

- Presidents George W. Bush, George H. W. Bush, John Adams, John Quincy Adams, Zachary Taylor, and Franklin D. Roosevelt could trace their family history to passengers on the *Mayflower*.

GLOSSARY

cargo: goods carried by a plane, train, or boat

chamber pot: a large bowl used as a toilet

charter: a piece of writing granting a person or group something, such as a piece of land

custom: a common practice among a group of people

merchant: having to do with the buying and selling of goods

New World: the name commonly used for the Americas during the era of exploration

pilot: someone who drives or steers a boat, plane, or car. Also, the act of driving or steering.

privacy: the state of being away from other people

religious: having to do with religion, or the faith a person follows

valuable: having great value

voyage: a trip, especially by ship

Books

Barber, Nicola. *Who Journeyed on the Mayflower?* Chicago, IL: Capstone Heinemann Library, 2014.

Cook, Peter, et al. *You Wouldn't Want to Sail the Seas!* San Diego, CA: Parfait Press, 2012.

Websites

Mayflower and the Mayflower Compact
www.plimoth.org/learn/just-kids/homework-help/mayflower-and-mayflower-compact
Read more about the *Mayflower's* voyage and the Mayflower Compact that was signed aboard it.

The First Thanksgiving: Tour the *Mayflower*
www.scholastic.com/scholastic_thanksgiving/voyage/tour.htm
What did the inside of the *Mayflower* look like? Check out this interactive website to find out!

Publisher's note to educators and parents: Our editors have carefully reviewed these websites to ensure that they are suitable for students. Many websites change frequently, however, and we cannot guarantee that a site's future contents will continue to meet our high standards of quality and educational value. Be advised that students should be closely supervised whenever they access the Internet.